BOOK 3

CLASSIC ROCK HITS
for TEENS

W9-AIO-432

7 GRADED SELECTIONS
FOR LATE INTERMEDIATE PIANISTS

ARRANGED BY DAN COATES

The *Classic Rock Hits for Teens* series presents carefully leveled, accessible arrangements for the teenage pianist. This series provides students with the opportunity to develop their technique and musicianship while performing popular pieces by their favorite musicians.

CONTENTS

Produced by
Alfred Music
P.O. Box 10003
Van Nuys, CA 91410-0003
alfred.com

Printed in USA.

ISBN-10: 1-4706-2331-5
ISBN-13: 978-1-4706-2331-9

Cover Images:
Lava Lamp: © Shutterstock.com / Adventure_Photo • Headphones: © Shutterstock.com / Alexander Demyanenko

DANCING IN THE MOONLIGHT

Words and Music by Sherman Kelly
Arr. Dan Coates

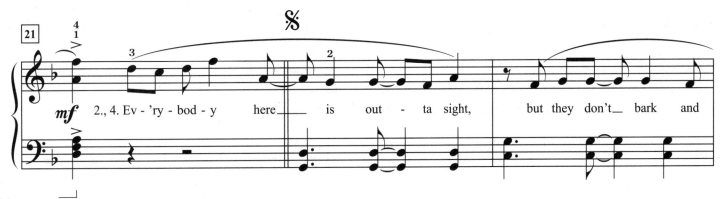

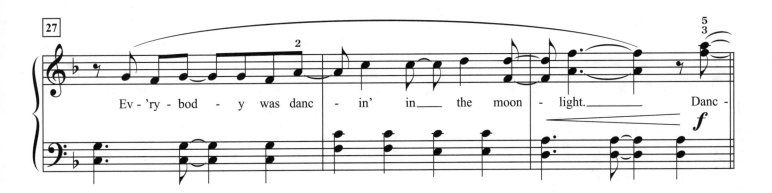

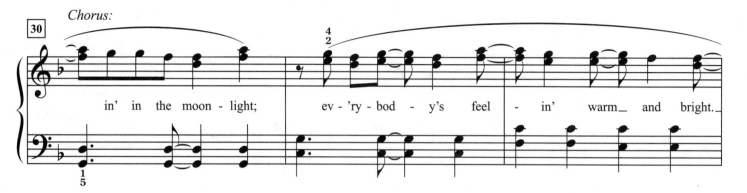

Chorus:

30 in' in the moon - light; ev - 'ry - bod - y's feel - in' warm_ and bright.

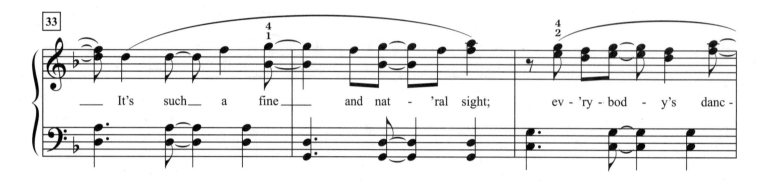

33 _ It's such_ a fine_ and nat - 'ral sight; ev - 'ry - bod - y's danc -

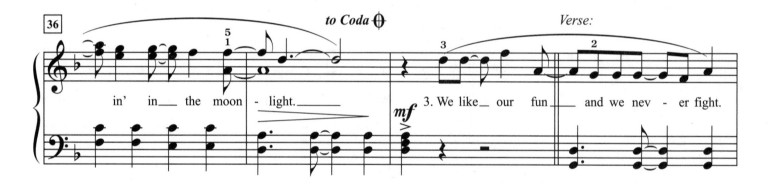

to Coda

Verse:

36 in' in_ the moon - light._ 3. We like_ our fun_ and we nev - er fight.

mf

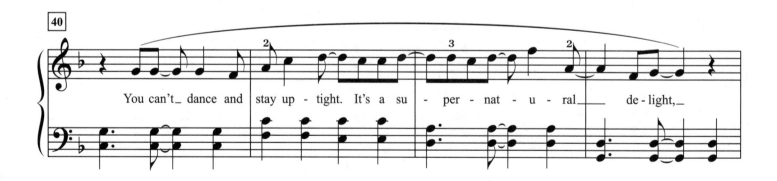

40 You can't_ dance and stay up - tight. It's a su - per - nat - u - ral_ de - light,_

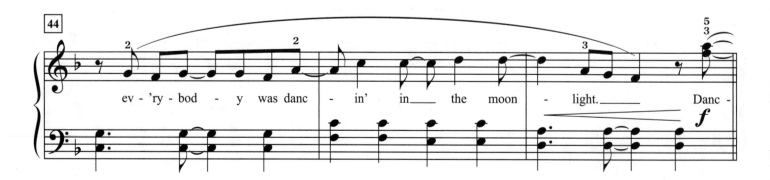

44 ev - 'ry - bod - y was danc - in' in_ the moon - light._ Danc -

f

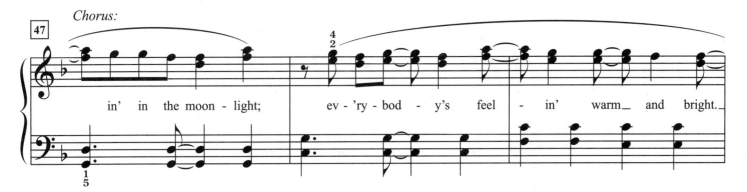

6

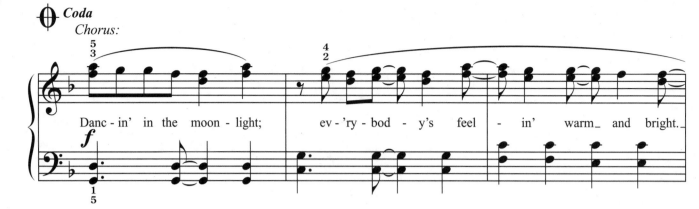

Coda
Chorus:

Danc-in' in the moon-light; ev-'ry-bod-y's feel - in' warm and bright.

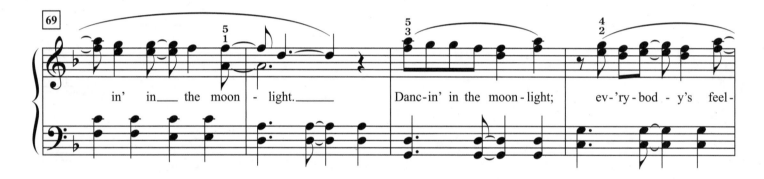

___ It's such___ a fine___ and nat - 'ral sight; ev-'ry-bod-y's danc-

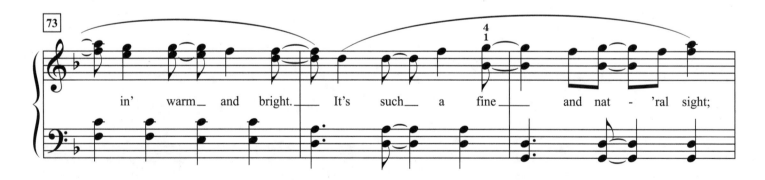

in' in___ the moon - light._____ Danc-in' in the moon-light; ev-'ry-bod-y's feel-

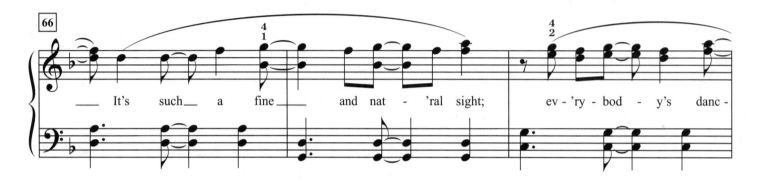

in' warm___ and bright.___ It's such___ a fine___ and nat - 'ral sight;

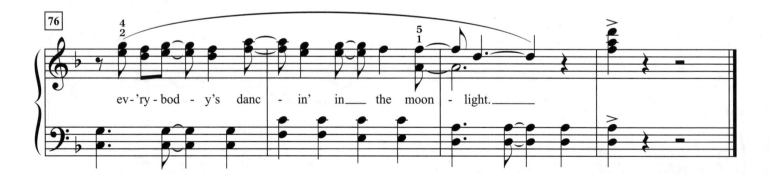

ev-'ry-bod - y's danc - in' in___ the moon - light._____

DO YOU FEEL LIKE WE DO

Words and Music by Peter Frampton,
John Siomos, Rick Willis and Mick Gallagher
Arr. Dan Coates

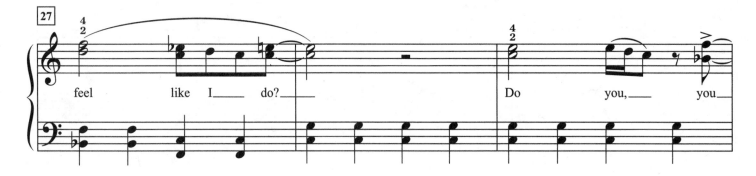

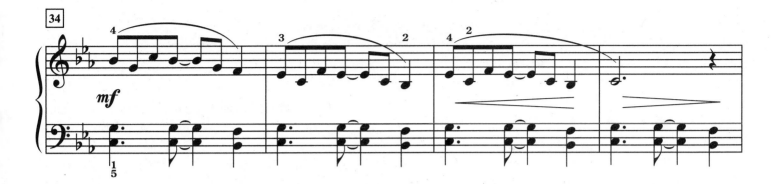

FAITHFULLY

Words and Music by Jonathan Cain
Arr. Dan Coates

Moderately slow

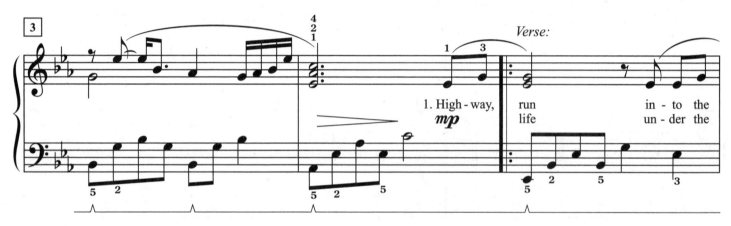

1. High - way,
run
in - to the
life
un - der the

mid - night___ sun.___
big - top___ world___

Wheels go 'round___ and 'round; you're on my mind.
We all need___ the clowns to make us smile.

Rest - less hearts
Through space and time,

sleep a - lone to - night,___
always an - oth - er___ show.___

12

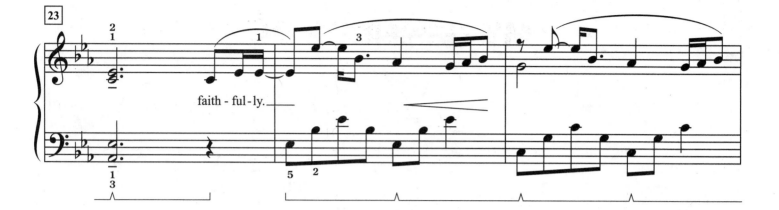

faith - ful - ly.

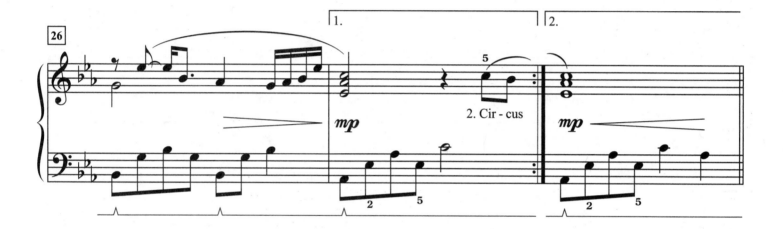

mp

2. Cir - cus

mp

f

Oh,_____ oh,_____

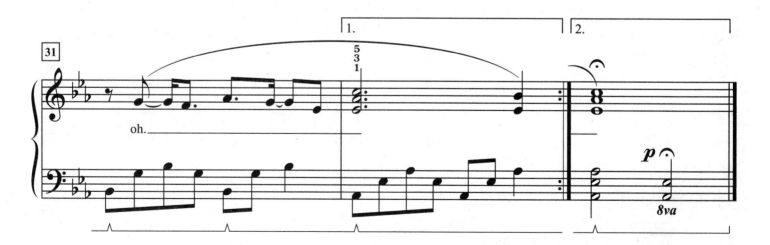

oh._____

p

8va

MY GENERATION

Words and Music by Peter Townshend
Arr. Dan Coates

Moderately, with a steady rock beat

People try to put us down,__ (Talk-in' 'bout my gen - er - a - tion.)

just be-cause we get a - round. (Talk-in' 'bout my gen - er - a - tion.)

Things they do look aw-ful cold.__ (Talk - in' 'bout my gen - er - a - tion.)

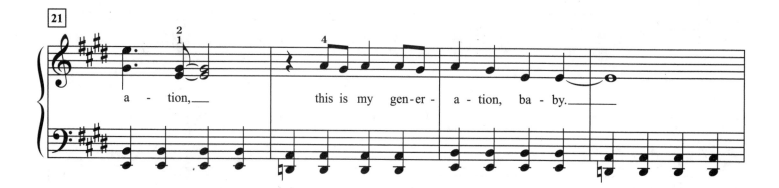

not tryin' to cause a big sen-sa-tion. *(Talk-in' 'bout my gen - er-a-tion.)* I'm

just talk-in' 'bout my gen - er-a-tion. *(Talk-in' 'bout my...)* This is my gen-er-

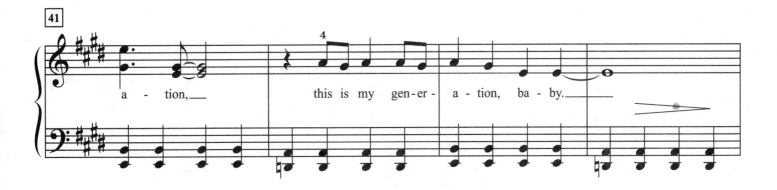

a - tion,___ this is my gen-er - a - tion, ba - by.___

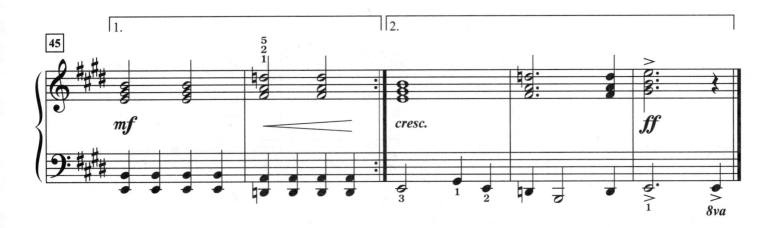

1.

2.

FOOL IN THE RAIN

Words and Music by John Paul Jones,
Jimmy Page and Robert Plant
Arr. Dan Coates

Moderately bright shuffle

light in your eye___ that keeps shin - ing, like a star that can't wait___ for the night.
bod - y is start - ing to quiv - er, and the palms of my hand's___ get - ting wet.

I hate to think I've been blind - ed, ba - by,
I got no rea - son to doubt___ you, ba - by,

why can't I see you to-night?____
it's all a ter-ri-ble mess.____ And the   And I'll

warmth of your smile_ starts a-burn-
run in the rain_ till I'm breath-

ing,   and the   thrill of your touch_ gives me fright.   And I'm
less,   when I'm   breath-less I'll run_ till   I   drop.   The

shak-ing so much,_ real-ly yearn   - ing,   why don't you show up and make it all right._
thoughts of a fool's_ kind of care - less,   I'm just a fool wait - ing on the wrong block.

to Coda ⊕

And if you

prom-ised your love___ so com-plete - ly, and you said you would al - ways be
stand in the rain___ on the cor - ner, I'll watch the peo-ple go shuff - ling down-

true. You swore that you nev - er would leave___ me, ba - by,___
town. An - oth-er ten min - utes, no long - er,

what ev - er hap-pened to you.___ And you thought it was on - ly in you,___ as you
and then I'm turn - ing a-round.___ And the clock on the wall's mov-ing slow-er, oh, my

wished all your dreams would come true.___ It ain't the first time, be - lieve
heart___ it sinks___ to the ground.___ And the___ storm that I thought would blow o -

___ me___ ba - by,___ I'm stand-ing here feel-ing blue.___
ver___ clouds the___ light of the love that I found.___

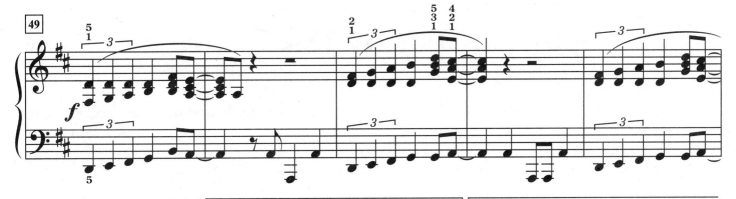

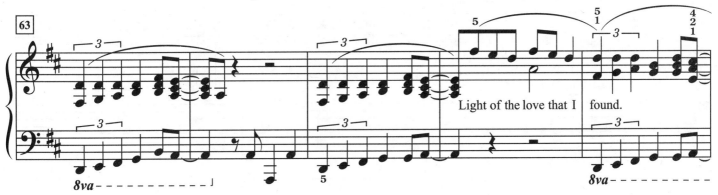

SATURDAY IN THE PARK

Words and Music by Robert Lamm
Arr. Dan Coates

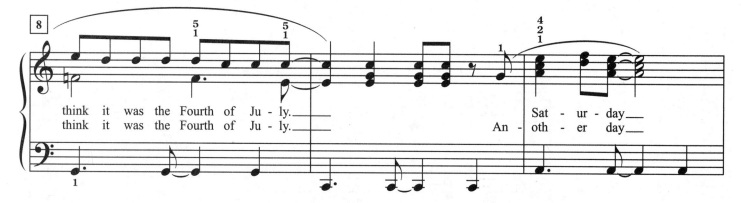

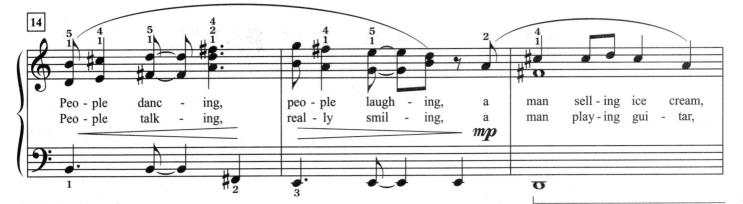

Peo - ple danc - ing, peo - ple laugh - ing, a man sell - ing ice cream,
Peo - ple talk - ing, real - ly smil - ing, a man play - ing gui - tar,

mp

sing - ing I - tal - ian songs. (Ei - cay va - re,
sing - ing___ for us all. Will you help___ him

cresc.

ei - se nar - de.) Can you dig___ it? Yes, I___ can.___ And I've been
change the world?___ Can you dig___ it? Yes, I___ can.___ And I've been

mf

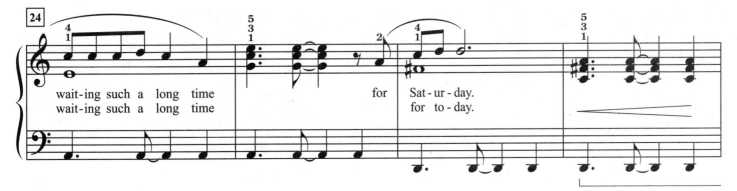

wait - ing such a long time for Sat - ur - day.
wait - ing such a long time for to - day.

1.

f

An -

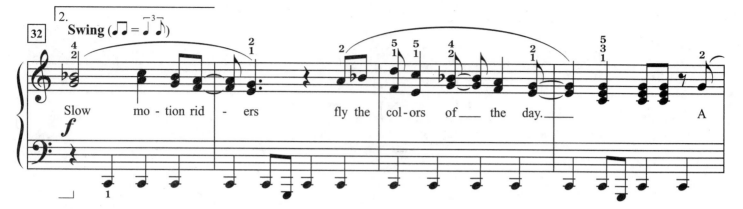

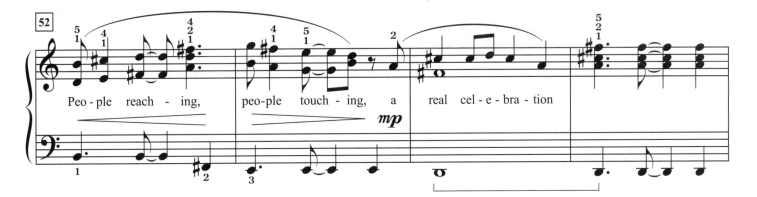

Peo - ple reach - ing, peo - ple touch - ing, a real cel - e - bra - tion

mp

wait - ing for__ us all. If you want__ it, real - ly want__ it,

cresc.

can you dig__ it? Yes, I__ can.__ And I've been wait - ing such a long time

mf

for the day, yeah,____ yeah, ooh,__ mm,

__ mm.____

f

8va - - - -

STAIRWAY TO HEAVEN

Words and Music by
Jimmy Page and Robert Plant
Arr. Dan Coates

Ooo,_____ ooo,_____ and she's buy - ing a stair - way to

heav - en. There's a sign on the wall, but she wants to be sure,__ 'cause you

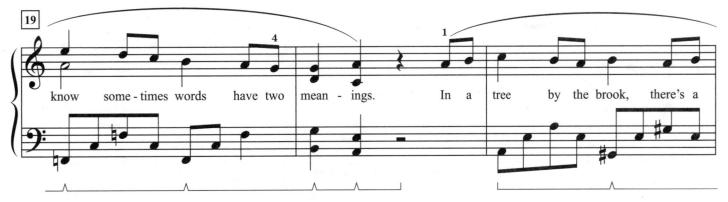

know some - times words have two mean - ings. In a tree by the brook, there's a

song - bird who sings,_ some - times all of our thoughts are mis - giv - en.

Ooo,_ it makes me won - der._____

It makes me won-der.   There's a

feel - ing I get when I look to the west,_ and my spir - it is cry-ing for
whis - pered that soon if we all call the tune,_ then the pip - er will lead us to

leav - ing. In my thoughts I have seen rings of smoke through the trees,_ and the
rea - son. And a new day will dawn for those who stand long,_ and the

voic - es of those who stand look - ing And it's
for - ests will ech - o with   laugh - ter.

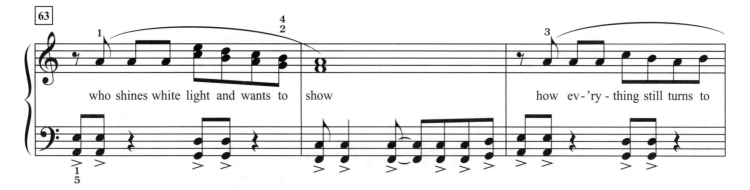

who shines white light and wants to show

how ev-'ry-thing still turns to

gold.

And if you lis-ten ver-y hard,

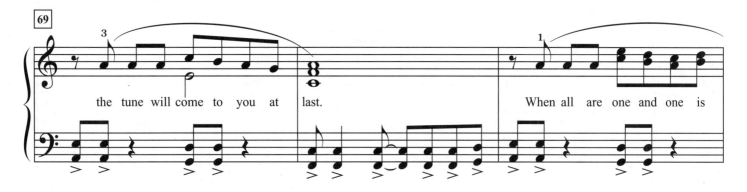

the tune will come to you at last.

When all are one and one is

all,

to be a rock and not to roll.

ff

Freely

And she's buy-ing a stair-way to heav-en.

mf *rit.* *mp*